THE OFFICIAL 2007
ASTON VILLA
ANNUAL

Compiled by Rob Bishop and Tricia Freeman

Special thanks to Gayner Monkton, Lorna McClelland
and Neville Williams Photography

A Grange Publication

© 2006. Published by Grange Communications Ltd., Edinburgh under licence
from Aston Villa Football Club plc. Printed in the EU.

ISBN 0-9550057-2-8

£6.99

Club Honours

EUROPEAN CUP
Winners: 1982
Quarter-finalists: 1982-83

EUROPEAN SUPER CUP
Winners: 1982-83

WORLD CLUBS CHAMPIONSHIP
Runners-up: 1982

INTERTOTO CUP
Winners: 2001

FOOTBALL LEAGUE
Champions: 1893-94, 1895-96, 1896-97, 1898-99,
1899-1900, 1909-10, 1980-81
Runners-up: 1888-89, 1902-03, 1907-08, 1910-11, 1912-13,
1913-14, 1930-31, 1932-33, 1989-90

PREMIERSHIP
Runners-up: 1992-93

DIVISION TWO
Champions: 1937-38, 1959-60

DIVISION THREE
Champions: 1971-72

FA CUP
Winners: 1887, 1895, 1897, 1905, 1913, 1920, 1957
Runners-up: 1892, 1924, 2000

LEAGUE CUP
Winners: 1961, 1975, 1977, 1994, 1996
Runners-up: 1963, 1971

FA YOUTH CUP
Winners: 1972, 1980, 2002
Runners-up: 2004

Contents

DAVIS

Steven Davis

2005-2006 Season Review

August

What a start – four goals in the first nine minutes of the opening match! Summer signing Kevin Phillips heads us into the lead after just three minutes and 12 seconds of his debut against Bolton Wanderers and Steven Davis is also on target in that frantic opening spell. But Bolton score twice, too, and it finishes as a 2-2 draw.

It's very much a mixed start to the new campaign. After drawing with the Trotters, Villa lose 1-0 at Manchester United before a Richard Hughes own goal earns a point in a 1-1 draw at Portsmouth.

While the lads are on their way to Fratton Park, new signing Milan Baros is being unveiled back at Villa Park following his £7m transfer from Liverpool. The Czech striker marks his debut the following Saturday with the only goal at home to Blackburn Rovers to ensure Villa's first win.

Apart from Baros, Villa also sign Dutch defender Wilfred Bouma from PSV Eindhoven, plus James Milner and Eirik Bakke on loan from Newcastle United and Leeds United respectively. That's a total of eight new arrivals, with Phillips, Patrik Berger, Aaron Hughes and Stuart Taylor having been snapped up during the close-season.

Premiership position: 8th

Kevin Phillips in full flight

September

It's a bad start for Bouma, whose debut coincides with a 4-0 defeat by West Ham at Upton Park. But James Milner follows in the footsteps of Phillips and Baros by scoring on his home debut in a 1-1 draw against Tottenham Hotspur – and three nights later Villa go goal crazy at the Causeway Stadium.

A cup upset looks certain when Wycombe Wanderers lead 3-1 at half-time in the second round of the Carling Cup, but the visitors end up 8-3 winners with two goals each from James Milner, Gareth Barry and Steven Davis, plus one from Milan Baros and a Clint Easton own goal.

The following Saturday, Luke Moore becomes the first player to score a Premiership goal against Chelsea this season when he opens the scoring just before half-time. Unfortunately, the Blues equalise almost immediately and go on to win 2-1.

Premiership position: 15th

Season Review

October

It's not the happiest of months as we suffer Premiership home defeats at the hands of Middlesbrough and Wigan Athletic and also go down 3-1 at Manchester City.

But one single result is enough to lift the spirits of the claret and blue faithful. A superb Kevin Phillips goal clinches a 1-0 victory over Birmingham City at St. Andrew's – the first time we have got the better of our fiercest rivals since their promotion to the top flight three years earlier.

Phillips also scores the only goal in a 1-0 Carling Cup home win over Burnley, a result which avenges Villa's 3-1 exit at Turf Moor 12 months earlier. Defender Mark Delaney makes his first appearance of the season against the Clarets after recovering from a knee injury.

Premiership position: 16th

November

Despite losing at home to Liverpool, Villa lift themselves away from the Premiership danger zone with back-to-back wins against Sunderland (3-1) and Charlton Athletic (1-0).

Kevin Phillips sets the ball rolling with a superb header against his former club at the Stadium of Light, the other goals coming from Gareth Barry and Milan Baros.

Then, a week later, Steven Davis is the match-winner against Charlton with a magnificent late goal, just when it looks like Villa will have to settle for a draw.

Don't mention penalties to Liam Ridgewell, by the way. The young defender concedes spot kicks against Liverpool and Sunderland – both of them harsh decisions – and then has another controversial decision go against him in the fourth round of the Carling Cup. He is adjudged to have handled against Doncaster Rovers at Belle Vue, even though it looks unintentional. The Yorkshire side go ahead from the penalty spot before completing a 3-0 victory which ends Villa's League Cup hopes for another season.

Team mates celebrate

Premiership position: 15th

December

We're off the mark! Gavin McCann and striker Juan Pablo Angel both end their scoring droughts by netting their first goals of the season on consecutive weekends. McCann's superb drive earns a 1-1 draw against Newcastle United at St. James' Park while Angel's late close-range effort has the same effect against Bolton Wanderers at the Reebok Stadium seven days later.

Villa's first home game for three weeks is a big let-down. Manchester United win 2-0 at Villa Park on the final Saturday before Christmas, thanks to goals from Ruud Van Nistelrooy and Wayne Rooney. But it's a much happier story over the festive season. Two goals from Milan Baros, plus further efforts from Mark Delaney and Juan Pablo Angel clinch a 4-0 Boxing Day victory over Everton, which is followed by another goal feast at Craven Cottage two nights later.

The game against Fulham finishes 3-3, Liam Ridgewell scoring twice for Villa to celebrate the birth of his baby son Luca the previous day. Luke Moore hits Villa's other goal, but neither side can make a breakthrough when Arsenal visit Villa Park on the final day of the year. The game against the Gunners ends goalless.

Premiership position: 13th.

January

Premiership position: 15th

Happy New Year! Villa make a flying start to 2006, beating West Bromwich Albion 2-1 at The Hawthorns. Steven Davis, who was 21 on New Year's Day, celebrates by heading the opening goal, with Milan Baros netting the winner from the penalty spot.

January, of course, is when the top clubs enter the FA Cup, and Gareth Barry's goal at Hull City ensures progress to the fourth round, where Villa beat Port Vale 3-1. Milan Baros scores two of the goals against the League One outfit, with David netting the other.

Apart from the win over Albion, David O'Leary's men have a mixed month in the Premiership. After losing at home to West Ham, they hang on for a goalless draw at Tottenham – where goalkeeper Thomas Sorensen is in magnificent form.

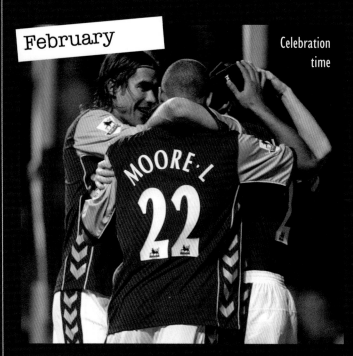

Celebration time

February

Luke Moore is in blistering form, the young striker scoring five goals in the space of three matches. His second half equaliser earns a richly-deserved 1-1 home draw against Chelsea and a few days later he becomes the first teenager to score a Premiership hat-trick for Villa, with Kevin Phillips also on target in an emphatic 4-0 win over Middlesbrough at The Riverside.

Then he scores with a fine header against Newcastle United at Villa Park, although that one isn't enough to prevent a 2-1 defeat by the Magpies.

The match against Newcastle is the day 19-year-old midfielder Craig Gardner makes his full debut, just after signing a contract designed to keep him at Villa Park until 2009.

In the fifth round of the FA Cup, Villa look set for progress until a fine Milan Baros goal is cancelled out by Micah Richards' stoppage time equaliser for Manchester City, which takes the tie to a replay.

Premiership position: 15th

Season Review

March

Without doubt, this is a month to forget. It starts well enough, a Milan Baros header securing a 1-0 home victory over Portsmouth, but goes downhill fast as Villa endure a nightmare in the North West!

One of the worst weeks in the club's recent history brings Premiership defeats at Blackburn Rovers and Everton – and in between, we also go out of the FA Cup, losing 2-1 at Manchester City in a fifth round replay. The only consolations for the boys in claret and blue are a late Steven Davis goal at the City of Manchester Stadium and a superb debut goal for Gabriel Agbonlahor at Goodison Park. The 19-year-old striker is given his big chance because Baros, Kevin Phillips and Juan Pablo Angel are all ruled out by injury or illness.

At least Villa stop the rot with a goalless draw against Fulham at Villa Park, although it's hardly a game worthy of the club's Family Fun Day.

Premiership position: 15th

Agbonlahor's debut goal

There's delight and despair for Villa as April produces both sunshine and showers.

The sunshine, both in the sky and on the pitch, comes on the day the lads beat Birmingham City 3-1 at Villa Park to complete a double over our rivals from the other side of the city.

It's a game to remember, too, Milan Baros putting us into an early lead before Chris Sutton equalises before half-time.

Then, on 58 minutes, Gary Cahill scores Villa's goal of the season with an acrobatic overhead kick which sends the Holte End into raptures. And a second Baros goal ensures that the celebrations continue for hours afterwards!

Villa also take a point from a goalless draw in another derby game against West Bromwich Albion, but otherwise nothing goes right as we suffer defeats at the hands of Arsenal, Wigan Athletic, Manchester City and Liverpool.

Premiership position: 16th

Thomas shows his delight

Gary's goal of the season

The final day of the season brings relegated Sunderland to Villa Park, the Black Cats having been condemned to the drop along with our Midland neighbours Blues and Albion.

After a run of three straight defeats, at least Villa end on a high note, a fine shot from Gareth Barry and a Liam Ridgewell header – his first goal at Villa Park – securing a 2-1 victory.

The other highlight of the month is the club's annual awards dinner. Steven Davis is voted Player of the Year, Young Player of the Year and Players' Young Player, while Gareth Barry receives the Players' Player of the Year award. Gary Cahill's spectacular volley against Birmingham City is voted Goal of the Season.

Final position: 16th

FIRST TEAM STATISTICS

	LEAGUE		CUPS	
	Apps	Gls	Apps	Gls
Gabriel AGBONLAHOR	3(6)	1	-	-
Juan Pablo ANGEL	12(19)	3	5(1)	-
Eirik BAKKE	8(6)	-	-	-
Milan BAROS	24(1)	8	5	4
Gareth BARRY	36	3	6	3
Patrik BERGER	3(5)	-	1	-
Wilfred BOUMA	20	-	1	-
Gary CAHILL	6(1)	1	1	-
Steven DAVIS	34(1)	4	7	4
Ulises DE LA CRUZ	4(3)	-	-(1)	-
Mark DELANEY	12	1	4	-
Eric DJEMBA-DJEMBA	-(4)	-	-	-
Craig GARDNER	3(5)	-	-(1)	-
Lee HENDRIE	7(9)	1	2(1)	-
Aaron HUGHES	35	-	6	-
Martin LAURSEN	1	-	-	-
Gavin McCANN	32	1	6	-
Olof MELLBERG	27	-	6	-
James MILNER	27	1	6	2
Luke MOORE	16(11)	8	3(2)	-
Kevin PHILLIPS	20(3)	4	2(2)	1
Liam RIDGEWELL	30(2)	5	4	-
Jlloyd SAMUEL	14(5)	-	5	-
Nobby SOLANO	2(1)	-	-	-
Thomas SORENSEN	36	-	7	-
Stuart TAYLOR	2	-	-	-
Peter WHITTINGHAM	4	-	-	-

Final Table

Team	P	W	D	L	F	A	W	D	L	F	A	Pts
		HOME					**AWAY**					
1. Chelsea	38	18	1	0	47	9	11	3	5	25	13	91
2. Manchester United	38	13	5	1	37	8	12	3	4	35	26	83
3. Liverpool	38	15	3	1	32	8	10	4	5	25	17	82
4. Arsenal	38	14	3	2	48	13	6	4	9	20	18	67
5. Tottenham Hotspur	38	12	5	2	31	16	6	6	7	22	22	65
6. Blackburn Rovers	38	13	3	3	31	17	6	3	10	20	25	63
7. Newcastle United	38	11	5	3	28	15	6	2	11	19	27	58
8. Bolton Wanderers	38	11	5	3	29	13	4	6	9	20	28	56
9. West Ham	38	9	3	7	30	25	7	4	8	22	30	55
10. Wigan Athletic	38	7	3	9	24	26	8	3	8	21	26	51
11. Everton	38	8	4	7	22	22	6	4	9	12	27	50
12. Fulham	38	13	2	4	31	21	1	4	14	17	37	48
13. Charlton Athletic	38	8	4	7	22	21	5	4	10	19	34	47
14. Middlesbrough	38	7	5	7	28	30	5	4	10	20	28	45
15. Manchester City	38	9	2	8	26	20	4	2	13	17	28	43
16. ASTON VILLA	**38**	**6**	**6**	**7**	**20**	**20**	**4**	**6**	**9**	**22**	**35**	**42**
17. Portsmouth	38	5	7	7	17	24	5	1	13	20	38	38
18. Birmingham City	38	6	5	8	19	20	2	5	12	9	30	34
19. West Bromwich A	38	6	2	11	21	24	1	7	11	10	34	30
20. Sunderland	38	1	4	14	12	37	2	2	15	14	32	15

Highs and Lows

HIGHEST HOME ATTENDANCE:
42,551 v Liverpool.

LOWEST HOME ATTENDANCE:
23,847 v Manchester City (FA Cup).

HIGHEST AWAY ATTENDANCE:
67,934 v Manchester United.

LOWEST AWAY ATTENDANCE:
5,365 v Wycombe Wanderers (Carling Cup).

BIGGEST WIN: 8-3 v Wycombe (Carling Cup)

BIGGEST DEFEAT: 5-0 v Arsenal (a)

QUICKFIRE KEVIN: Kevin Phillips scored Villa's fastest goal of the season, heading home after three minutes and 12 seconds of the opening day match at home to Bolton.

DEBUT BOYS
11 players made their Villa debuts last season:
Aaron Hughes v Bolton Wanderers (h)
Kevin Phillips v Bolton Wanderers (h)
Milan Baros v Blackburn Rovers (h)
Patrik Berger as sub v Blackburn (h)
Wilfred Bouma v West Ham (a)
James Milner v West Ham (a)
Gary Cahill v Wycombe, Carling Cup (a)
Eirik Bakke as sub v Middlesbrough (h)
Stuart Taylor v Manchester City (a)
Craig Gardner as sub v Everton (h)
Gabriel Agbonlahor v Everton (a)

ON THE SPOT
Villa's 2005-06 penalties:
Gareth Barry v Wycombe Wanderers (Carling Cup, a) - SCORED
Gareth Barry v Newcastle United (a) - MISSED
Milan Baros v West Bromwich Albion (a) - SCORED
Milan Baros v Newcastle United (a) – SAVED
Gareth Barry v Sunderland (h) - SAVED

RESULTS AT A GLANCE

Date	Opponents	Result	Scorers
Aug 13	BOLTON WANDERERS	2-2	Phillips, Davis
Aug 22	Manchester United	0-1	
Aug 23	Portsmouth	1-1	R Hughes (og)
Aug 27	BLACKBURN ROVERS	1-0	Baros
Sep 12	West Ham United	0-4	
Sep 17	TOTTENHAM HOTSPUR	1-1	Milner
Sep 20	Wycombe (LC2)	8-3	Barry 2, Milner 2, Davis 2, Baros, Easton (og)
Sep 24	Chelsea	1-2	Moore
Oct 2	MIDDLESBROUGH	2-3	Moore, Davis
Oct 16	Birmingham City	1-0	Phillips
Oct 22	WIGAN ATHLETIC	0-2	
Oct 25	BURNLEY (LC3)	1-0	Phillips
Oct 31	Manchester City	1-3	Ridgewell
Nov 5	LIVERPOOL	0-2	
Nov 19	Sunderland	3-1	Phillips, Barry, Baros
Nov 26	CHARLTON ATHLETIC	1-0	Davis
Nov 29	Doncaster Rovers (LC4)	0-3	
Dec 3	Newcastle United	1-1	McCann
Dec 10	Bolton Wanderers	1-1	Angel
Dec 17	MANCHESTER UNITED	0-2	
Dec 26	EVERTON	4-0	Baros 2, Delaney, Angel
Dec 28	Fulham	3-3	Moore, Ridgewell 2
Dec 31	ARSENAL	0-0	
Jan 2	West Bromwich Albion	2-1	Davis, Baros pen
Jan 7	Hull City (FAC3)	1-0	Barry
Jan 14	WEST HAM UNITED	1-2	Hendrie
Jan 21	Tottenham Hotspur	0-0	
Jan 28	PORT VALE (FAC4)	3-1	Baros 2, Davis
Feb 1	CHELSEA	1-1	Moore
Feb 4	Middlesbrough	4-0	Moore 3, Phillips
Feb 11	NEWCASTLE UNITED	1-2	Moore
Feb 19	MAN CITY (FAC5)	1-1	Baros
Feb 25	Charlton Athletic	0-0	
Mar 4	PORTSMOUTH	1-0	Baros
Mar 11	Blackburn Rovers	0-2	
Mar 14	Man City (FAC5 replay)	1-2	Davis
Mar 18	Everton	1-4	Agbonlahor
Mar 25	FULHAM	0-0	
Apr 1	Arsenal	0-5	
Apr 9	WEST BROM ALBION	0-0	
Apr 16	BIRMINGHAM CITY	3-1	Baros 2, Cahill
Apr 18	Wigan Athletic	2-3	Angel, Ridgewell
Apr 22	MANCHESTER CITY	0-1	
Apr 29	Liverpool	1-3	Barry
May 7	SUNDERLAND	2-1	Barry, Ridgewell

Magic Moments

Even in a disappointing season, there were still moments to savour for Villa's players. See if you agree with our choices...

Gary Cahill in action

GARY CAHILL
The young defender's spectacular goal in the 3-1 home victory over Birmingham City was arguably the most satisfying moment of Villa's season. Leaping into the air, he produced an acrobatic scissor-kick which left goalkeeper Maik Taylor clutching at thin air. It was just like watching Brazil!

GAVIN McCANN
Less spectacular than Cahill's wonder goal, but technically more perfect, Gavin's shot from outside the penalty area never left the ground as it flew inside the post. The build-up, featuring a superb pass from Lee Hendrie, was also pretty impressive.

LUKE MOORE
Just nine days short of his 20th birthday, Luke became the first teenager to score a Premiership hat-trick for Villa with three well-taken goals in a 4-0 triumph at Middlesbrough.

KEVIN PHILLIPS
Take your pick from his header after barely three minutes of the opening day match against Bolton – or the precise left foot shot which secured our first Premiership victory over Blues!

THOMAS SORENSEN
Our Danish goalkeeper made some fine saves, including five outstanding ones in a single afternoon as Villa held on for a goalless draw against Tottenham at White Hart Lane.

STEVEN DAVIS
The Northern Ireland international doesn't often score very many with his head, so his headed goal in the 2-1 win at West Brom was a perfect way to see in the New Year and celebrate his 21st birthday the previous day!

MILAN BAROS
The former Liverpool striker scored a dozen goals in his debut campaign at Villa Park – and none was more pleasing to the Villa faithful than the one which clinched a 3-1 victory and the "double" over Birmingham City!

15

Aston Martin!

Behind every successful football team, there's a good manager – and they don't come much better than Martin O'Neill.

Villa's boss knows all about winning trophies. As a clever midfielder in his playing days, he helped Nottingham Forest to the League Championship and two European Cup triumphs.

As a manager, he has guided Leicester City into the Premiership and then into the UEFA Cup before winning seven trophies in five years with Scottish giants Celtic.

Now he is bidding to bring the glory days back to Villa Park, and there's no doubt that Villa fans have taken him to their hearts.

Nearly 1,000 supporters turned up to welcome him when he was appointed as successor to David O'Leary and they are convinced the club have landed a genuine winner – even if it takes time.

O'Neill's managerial mentor is the legendary Brian Clough, who was his boss in the days when Forest ruled Europe.

And apart from picking up a lot of his former manager's astute methods, he is also one of the most passionate men in football.

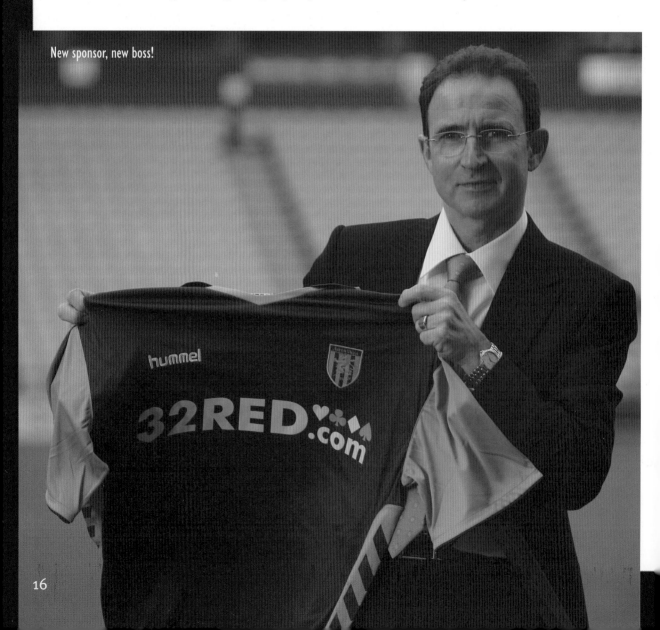

New sponsor, new boss!

Chairman Doug Ellis is delighted with Villa's new manager

Hero's welcome! Martin O'Neill arrives at Villa Park

You only have to watch him yelling instructions from the touchline to realise that. He is very ambitious, too.

"I think everyone is aware of the history of this club," he said. "Trying to restore those days of fantastic glory seems a long way off. But why not try?

"It's nearly 25 years since Villa won the European Cup. We're a long way from that at the moment – but that's the dream."

If you put the first part of Villa's name and the manager's Christian name together, you've got a famous sport car – Aston Martin. Here's to life in the fast lane!

One moment doesn't make a season, but this was, without doubt, the enduring image of Villa's 2005-06 campaign.

Young defender Gary Cahill leapt into the air and unleashed a spectacular scissor-kick which flew past Birmingham City goalkeeper Maik Taylor and into the net.

Villa were back in front against Blues – and they went on to complete a 3-1 Villa Park victory which gave them a double over their Second City rivals.

Describing his acrobatic strike, Gary explained: "I just saw the ball pop into the air. If I'd headed it, I don't think I would have got much power on it. So I tried a volley and thankfully it ended up in the net.

"I wasn't really aware how good it looked at the time. But one of our staff showed me a video of it on his laptop in the dressing room and I'm really proud of it. It's one I'll remember for a long, long time."

Not surprisingly, it was voted Villa's Goal of the Season, and the young defender was delighted when it was featured in the club's *Claret & Blue* magazine. We make no apologies for reproducing it here for Gary and Villa fans to savour over and over again!

A BAROS DOZEN!

Never mind a Baker's Dozen – which actually means 13 – Villa were treated to a genuine Baros Dozen in 2005-06.

On his own admission, Milan Baros didn't have the best of debut seasons after swapping the red of Liverpool for the claret and blue of Villa and was plagued by a series of niggling injuries.

Even so, the Czech international striker still had the distinction of being Villa's leading marksman with 12 goals. Here's how he scored them…

BLACKBURN ROVERS (h)
Peter Whittingham plays the ball forward from the half-way line and Kevin Phillips' deft pass sets up Baros for a low past goalkeeper Brad Friedel from 15 yards.

WYCOMBE (a)
A simple close-range conversion following a fine run and cross by Aaron Hughes – and Villa, having been 3-1 down, are on their way to a resounding 8-3 Carling Cup victory.

SUNDERLAND (a)
Luke Moore flicks on Gavin McCann's probing pass for Baros to pick his spot with a rising drive past advancing goalkeeper Ben Alnwick.

EVERTON (h)
The Czech striker admits he handled the ball before flicking it over Nigel Martyn for Villa's opening goal in a 4-0 Boxing Day victory.

EVERTON (h)
No arguments this time as he converts an Aaron Hughes centre at close range for the final goal in a fabulous festive victory over the Merseysiders.

WEST BROM (a)
A calmly converted penalty secures victory at The Hawthorns after Gareth Barry's fiercely-struck free-kick is handled in the area by former Villa defender Steve Watson.

Baros is chased by Sunderland's Andy Welsh   Baros celebrates his goal!

Baros celebrates with his team mates

7

PORT VALE (h)
A neat touch from substitute Kevin Phillips – his first contact with the ball – paves the way for a hard, low shot to give Villa the lead in their fourth round FA Cup-tie against the Valiants.

8

PORT VALE (h)
James Milner's right wing corner is headed on by skipper Olof Mellberg and Baros times his run to perfection to head home at the far post.

9

MANCHESTER CITY (h)
A stunning 15-yard drive past former Villa 'keeper David James in the fifth round of the Cup, after Steven Davis wins the ball and provides an astute pass through the middle.

PORTSMOUTH (h)
A simple close-range header from James Milner's left wing free-kick after Pompey's defenders make the big mistake of leaving him unmarked in the danger zone.

BIRMINGHAM CITY (h)
Superbly controlling a centre from Aaron Hughes, Baros is left with the simple task of firing past goalkeeper Maik Taylor from eight yards.

Baros and Birmingham's Olivier Tebily jump for the ball

12

BIRMINGHAM CITY (h)
A delightful build up involving Juan Pablo Angel and James Milner creates space for a right-foot angled shot beyond Taylor and into the far corner.

Villans
ON THE CARDS

VILLANS

32RED.com

Thomas **Sorensen**

Born: FREDERECIA, DENMARK, 12/06/76
Position: GOALKEEPER
Signed: AUG 2003
Debut: PORTSMOUTH (a) 16/08/03, Premiership
Previous clubs: ODENSE BK, SUNDERLAND

VILLANS

hummel

Stuart **Taylor**

Born: ROMFORD, 28/11/80
Position: GOALKKEEPER
Signed: JUNE 2005
Debut: MANCHESTER CITY (a) 31/10/05, Premiership
Previous club: ARSENAL

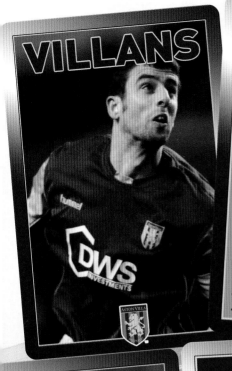

VILLANS

Born: HAVERFORDWEST, 13/05/76
Position: RIGHT-BACK
Signed: MARCH, 1999
Debut: NOTTINGHAM FOREST (h) 24/09/99, Premiership
Previous club: CARDIFF CITY

Mark **Delaney**

VILLANS

VILLANS

Born: AMNCHARAD, SWEDEN, 03/09/77
Position: CENTRAL DEFENDER
Signed: JULY, 2001
Debut: TOTTENHAM (a) 18/08/01, Premiership
Previous clubs: DAGEFORS, AIK STOCKHOLM, RACING SANTANDER

Olof **Mellberg**

Born: PIQULUCHO, ECUADOR, 08/02/74
Position: RIGHT-BACK
Signed: AUGUST, 2002
Debut: LIVERPOOL (h) 18/08/02, Premiership
Previous clubs: DEPORTO QUITTO, HIBERNIAN

Ulises **De La Cruz**

VILLANS

Born: SILKEBORG, DENMARK, 26/07/76
Position: CENTRAL DEFENDER
Signed: MAY, 2004
Debut: SOUTHAMPTON (h) 14/08/04, Premiership
Previous clubs: SILKEBORG, VERONA, PARMA, AC MILAN

Martin **Laursen**

23

VILLANS

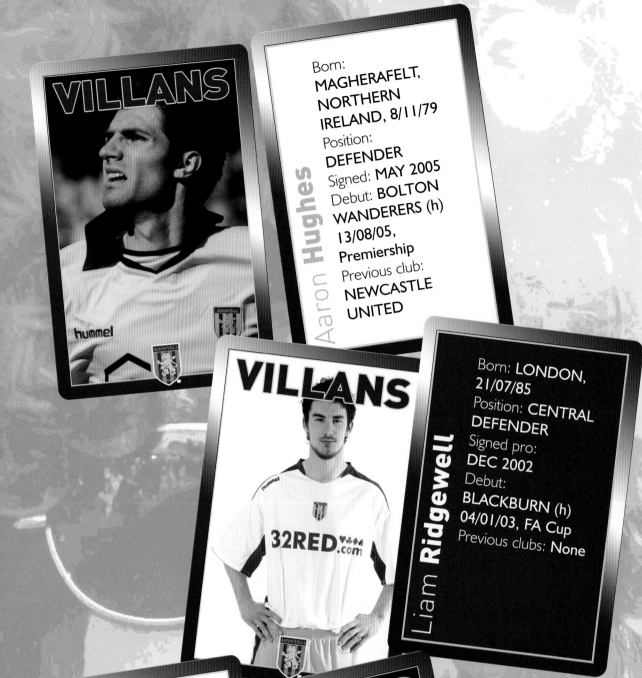

Born: MAGHERAFELT, NORTHERN IRELAND, 8/11/79

Position: DEFENDER

Signed: MAY 2005

Debut: BOLTON WANDERERS (h) 13/08/05, Premiership

Previous club: NEWCASTLE UNITED

Aaron **Hughes**

VILLANS

32RED.com

Born: LONDON, 21/07/85

Position: CENTRAL DEFENDER

Signed pro: DEC 2002

Debut: BLACKBURN (h) 04/01/03, FA Cup

Previous clubs: None

Liam **Ridgewell**

Born: SHEFFIELD, 19/12/85

Position: DEFENDER

Signed pro: DEC 2003

Debut: WYCOMBE WANDERERS (a) 20/09/05, League Cup

Previous clubs: None

Gary **Cahill**

VILLANS

Born: **TRINIDAD, 29/03/81**
Position: **LEFT-BACK**
Signed pro: **JAN 1999**
Debut: **CHESTER CITY (h) 21/09/99, League Cup**
Previous club: **CHARLTON ATHLETIC**

Jlloyd **Samuel**

VILLANS

VILLANS

VILLAN

Born: **BIRMINGHAM, 18/05/77**
Position: **MIDFIELDER**
Signed pro: **JULY 1994**
Debut: **QPR (a) 23/12/95, Premiership**
Previous clubs: **None**

Lee **Hendrie**

Born: **BLACKPOOL, 10/01/78**
Position: **MIDFIELDER**
Signed: **JULY 2003**
Debut: **PORTSMOUTH (a) 16/08/03, Premiership**
Previous clubs: **EVERTON, SUNDERLAND**

Gavin **McCann**

Born: **CAMEROON, 04/05/81**
Position: **MIDFIELDER**
Signed: **JAN 2005**
Debut: **FULHAM (a) 02/02/05, Premiership**
Previous clubs: **NANTES, MANCHESTER UNITED**

Eric **Djemba-Djemba**

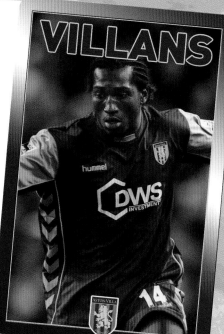

VILLANS

VILLANS

Born: PRAGUE, CZECH REPUBLIC, 10/11/73

Position: MIDFIELDER

Signed: JULY 2005

Debut: BLACKBURN ROVERS (h) 17/09/05, Premiership

Previous clubs: SLAVIA PRAGUE, BORUSSIA DORTMUND, LIVERPOOL, PORTSMOUTH

Patrik **Berger**

VILLANS

Born: HASTINGS, 23/02/81

Position: MIDFIELDER

Signed pro: FEB 1998

Debut: SHEFFIELD WEDNESDAY (a) 02/05/98, Premiership

Previous club: BRIGHTON

Gareth **Barry**

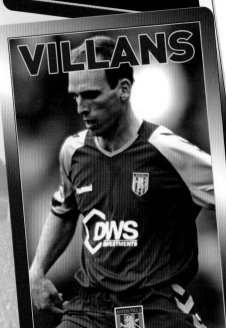

VILLANS

Born: VANNES, FRANCE, 23/02/80

Position: MIDFIELDER

Signed: AUG 2004

Debut: QPR (h) 22/09/04, League Cup

Previous club: NANTES

Mathieu **Berson**

VILLANS

2R

Born: BALLYMENA, NORTHERN IRELAND, 01/01/85
Position: MIDFIELDER
Signed pro: JAN 2002
Debut: NORWICH CITY (a) 18/09/04, Premiership
Previous clubs: None

Steven **Davis**

VILLANS

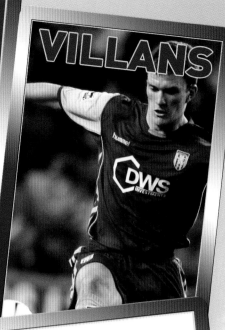

Born: NUNEATON, 08/09/84
Position: MIDFIELDER
Signed pro: OCT 2002
Debut: NEWCASTLE UNITED (a) 21/04/03, Premiership
Previous clubs: None

Peter **Whittingham**

VILLAN

Born: BIRMINGHAM, 25/11/86
Position: MIDFIELDER
Signed pro: JAN 2005
Debut: EVERTON (h) 26/12/05, Premiership
Previous clubs: None

Craig **Gardner**

VILLANS

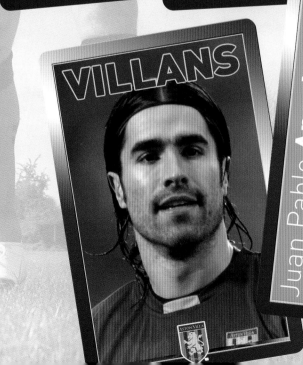

Born: MEDELLIN, COLOMBIA, 24/10/75
Position: STRIKER
Signed: JAN 2001
Debut: MANCHESTER UNITED (a) 20/01/01, Premiership
Previous clubs: NACIONAL, RIVER PLATE

Juan Pablo **Angel**

VILLANS

Born: CZECH REPUBLIC, 28/10/81
Position: STRIKER
Signed: AUG 2005
Debut: BLACKBURN ROVERS (h) 27/09/05, Premiership
Previous clubs: BANIK OSTRAVA, RIVER PLATE

Milan **Baros**

VILLANS

Born: HITCHIN, 25/07/73
Position: STRIKER
Signed: JUNE 2005
Debut: BOLTON WANDERERS (h) 13/08.05, Premiership
Previous clubs: WATFORD, SUNDERLAND, SOUTHAMPTON

Kevin **Phillips**

VILLANS

Born: BIRMINGHAM, 13/02/86
Position: STRIKER
Signed pro: FEB 2003
Debut: BIRMINGHAM CITY (h) 22/02/04, Premiership
Previous clubs: **None**

Luke **Moore**

VILLANS

Born: BIRMINGHAM, 13/10/86
Position: STRIKER
Signed pro: FEB 2005
Debut: EVERTON (a) 18/03/05
Previous clubs: None

Gabriel **Agbonlahor**

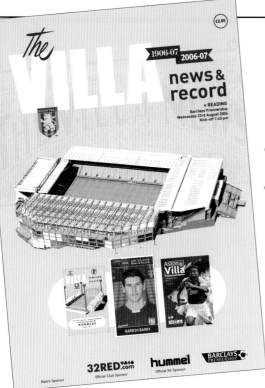

100 not out!

– although we decided it was more fitting to show the ground as it is now rather than how it was half a century ago!

Inside each issue, there's a focus on various periods throughout the programme's history, looking at how Villa's major triumphs and other significant events were covered over the course of 100 years.

Those early issues are priceless and over the course of the next few years, a full set of the Centenary series is likely to become a collector's item.

Make sure you tell mum and dad to get a copy and help you build your collection. Match day at Villa Park isn't the same without the **Villa News & Record!**

The 2006-07 season is a very special time for the **Villa News & Record** – it's the programme's 100th birthday!

Way back on 1st September, 1906, the club produced a programme for the first time, and a century later the publication is still going strong.

That first issue cost one penny, which was less than 1p in today's money. These days it's £2.50, but that's still great value because it's packed with interesting features and superb photos of your favourite players – and is one of the cheapest programmes in the country.

To celebrate our Centenary, we have combined the traditional with the modern for the look of this season's programme.

The cover, compiled by graphic designer Nadine Lees, is based on a theme which was introduced in 1949 and continued right through the 1950s and into the 60s.

As you can see, it once again features a picture of Villa Park

You've won!

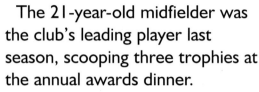

Steven Davis didn't know he was Villa's Player of the Year – until he received a text message telling him so!

The 21-year-old midfielder was the club's leading player last season, scooping three trophies at the annual awards dinner.

He also established himself as a regular in the Northern Ireland team, helping his country for a famous victory over England in Belfast.

Yet he started the campaign just grateful to be in the team – and wasn't even around when it was time to collect his end-of-term awards!

By the time it was revealed that he had won his trio of trophies – Player of the Year, Young Player of the Year and Players' Young Player of the Year – Steven was tucked up in bed.

"I'd been having a lot of pain and discomfort in my mouth after one of my fillings came out," he

"The award was open to all sports people, so I was really honoured to win it"

explained. "The club doctor advised me to get home to bed – but at least the other lads sent me text messages to tell me what I'd won!

While he was disappointed to miss the presentations, at least Steven was presented with his trophies before Villa's final home game against Sunderland.

And they weren't the only things he won in 2005-06. He was also voted Young Footballer of the Year by BBC Midlands, as well as receiving the first Belfast Telegraph George Best Breakthrough Award.

Best, who had died a few months earlier, was one of the greatest footballers of all time — and, like Steven, he was a Northern Ireland international.

"The award was open to all sports people, so I was really honoured to win it," said the young Villa star. "Perhaps the organisers felt it would be appropriate that the first recipient should be a footballer.

"I was immensely proud. It's one thing to admire George Best but quite another to win an award named after him."

For all his success, Davis admits he was just happy to be in the team at the start of the season.

"You can never take anything for granted in football," he says. "I'd made my debut the previous year and by the end of that season I'd played quite a few games. But I still had doubts about whether I'd be picked for the opening game."

Not only was he selected, he began with a bang, scoring in a 2-2 draw against Bolton, and went on to play more than 40 league and cup games, hitting eight goals.

Only one of them was a header, when he opened the scoring in a 2-1 win against Albion at The Hawthorns, but it was a perfect present for his 21st birthday 24 hours earlier, on New Year's Day.

He knows, though, that time never stands still, which is why he was delighted when the club offered him a new contract which secures his future at Villa Park until the summer of 2009.

"I've always been happy here," he says. "More than anything, I would love to progress with this club and help them win major honours.

"It's always nice to be recognised for your efforts, so it was a great honour to receive those awards last season. But I'd happily swap them for success with the team."

31

AGBONLAHOR

Gabriel Agbonlahor

QUICK QUIZ

Here's a chance to test your knowledge of Villa. See how many of these questions you can answer – then test your friends to see if they can beat your score!

1. Who was Villa's top scorer last season – and how many goals did he score?

2. Which team did Villa beat 3-2 to go top of the Premiership in October 2001?

3. Who scored Villa's only hat-trick last season?

4. And who was the previous player to score a Premiership hat-trick for the club, in 1998?

5. Steven Davis supported which Scottish club when he was a boy?

6. Name the three players who scored on their Villa debuts last season. Here's a clue – two were at home and one was away.

7. Who did Villa beat to win the European Cup in 1982?

8. Three former Villa Academy players made their first team debuts last season. Can you name them?

9. Which defender did Villa sign from PSV Eindhoven in the summer of 2005?

10. Who is Villa's record signing – and how much did he cost?

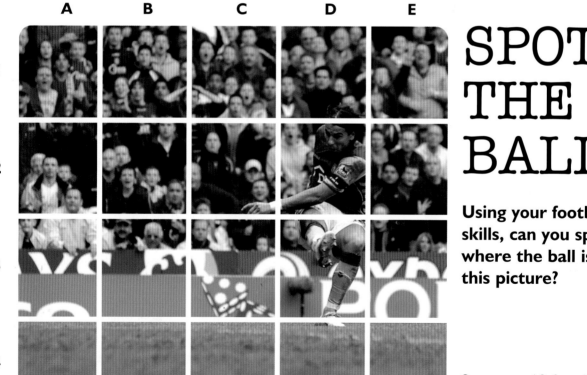

SPOT THE BALL

Using your football skills, can you spot where the ball is in this picture?

See page 60 for the answers.

33

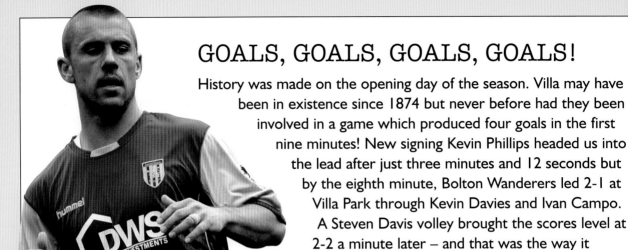

GOALS, GOALS, GOALS, GOALS!

History was made on the opening day of the season. Villa may have been in existence since 1874 but never before had they been involved in a game which produced four goals in the first nine minutes! New signing Kevin Phillips headed us into the lead after just three minutes and 12 seconds but by the eighth minute, Bolton Wanderers led 2-1 at Villa Park through Kevin Davies and Ivan Campo. A Steven Davis volley brought the scores level at 2-2 a minute later – and that was the way it stayed.

WOULD YOU

Amazing facts about the 2005-06 season

HAT-TRICK OF HAT-TRICKS

Another piece of club history was created when three players scored in consecutive home debuts.

After Phillips had set the trend against Bolton, Milan Baros continued it with an 11th minute winner against Blackburn – and then on-loan James Milner was on target in the fourth minute of his home debut against Tottenham Hotspur. Gabriel Agbonlahor also scored on his debut later in the season, a consolation goal in a 4-1 defeat by Everton at Goodison Park.

A TEAM OF SUBS

Villa could have fielded a full team of players who made their debuts for the club last season. The 11 – in order of appearance! – were Aaron Hughes, Kevin Phillips, Milan Baros, Patrik Berger, Wilfred Bouma, James Milner, Gary Cahill, Eirik Bakke, Stuart Taylor, Craig Gardner and Gabriel Agbonlahor.

SEVENTH HEAVEN IN SECOND HALF

Villa's 8-3 win at Wycombe in the second round of the Carling Cup equalled a record in the competition. The only previous time 11 goals had been scored in a League Cup-tie (not including penalty shoot-outs!) was when Leyton Orient beat Chester 9-2 in 1962. And never before had a visiting team come back from a 3-1 down at half-time to score seven second half goals. It was only the third time Villa had scored eight times in a competitive away match, the other occasions being at Clapton Orient (8-0 in 1929) and at Leicester City (8-3 in 1932).

AT THE DOUBLE

Villa completed only two "doubles" last season – but one of them was particularly sweet. The two wins over Birmingham City (1-0 at St. Andrew's, 3-1 at Villa Park) were our first against Blues in the Premiership. The other team we beat twice were Sunderland (3-1 away, 2-1 at home).

BELIEVE IT?

ON AND OFF

The City of Manchester Stadium was certainly an unlucky venue for Villa. The unfortunate Patrik Berger replaced Jlloyd Samuel at half-time in the Premiership match away to City but then picked up a knee injury which forced him to be substituted by Eric Djemba-Djemba after 75 minutes.

And in the same match, goalkeeper Stuart Taylor learned he would be making his debut just minutes before kick-off – after Thomas Sorensen injured his back during the warm-up!

Luke Moore, meanwhile, went on as an 80th minute substitute for Milan Baros in the goalless draw at Tottenham – and was replaced by Samuel five minutes later! Villa made the switch when they were forced to reorganise after Gareth Barry was sent off.

I'M JUST A TEENAGE HAT-TRICK HERO!

Luke Moore is an unassuming young man who doesn't have a great deal to say about himself. He's a footballer who prefers to do his talking on the pitch – and he certainly did that when Villa went down by The Riverside last season.

Still a week short of his 20th birthday at the time, Moore was in lethal form as he became the first teenager to score a Premiership hat-trick for Villa.

His three well-taken goals – plus a header from Kevin Phillips – made him very much a "yellow peril" on Teesside as Villa romped to an emphatic 4-0 victory.

Moore opened the scoring in the 18th minute with a left-foot shot after Phillips had cleverly flicked Jlloyd Samuel's centre into his path.

Then, after Phillips had made it 2-0, the youngster calmly converted at close range on 62 minutes following a surging Steven Davis run and a low cross from Gareth Barry.

Luke celebrates with Kevin Phillips and James Milner

36

Luke celebrates, with Kevin Phillips chasing him

And he rounded off the scoring two minutes from time by clipping the ball over goalkeeper Mark Schwarzer following a brilliant pass from Davis.

Typically, though, Luke doesn't intend to get carried away by his success, even though he finished the season with eight league goals – the same number as £7m Czech striker Milan Baros.

"Like any striker, I just love scoring goals," he said. "But it would be wrong for me to be anything but level-headed because this is just the start for me.

"I want to achieve so much. Last season was only my second year as a pro and I just want to improve."

Up to the end of last season, Luke was one of only six players who had scored league hat-tricks for Villa since the formation of the Premiership in 1992-93. **Dean Saunders** was the first – with the help of two penalties – against Swindon Town in 1994, while **Tommy Johnson** helped himself to three goals in a 7-1 demolition of Wimbledon 12 months later.

Savo Milosevic joined the hat-trick club with a treble against Coventry City the following season and then **Dwight Yorke** hit three against Newcastle United at St. James' Park – only to have another effort disallowed and finish on the losing side!

But there was no such misfortune for **Dion Dublin**.

Dublin's hat-trick at Southampton in 1998 helped Villa to a 4-1 win which extended their unbeaten league run to 12 matches – the club's best-ever start to a season.

Three other players, meanwhile, have scored Villa hat-tricks in cup-ties during the Premiership years – **Stan Collymore** in the UEFA Cup, **Benito Carbone** in the FA Cup and **JPA** in the League Cup.

VILLA'S PREMIER HAT-TICKS

DEAN SAUNDERS
Swindon Town (h) 5-0
February 1994

TOMMY JOHNSON
Wimbledon (h) 7-1
February 1995

SAVO MILOSEVIC
Coventry City (h) 4-1
December 1995

DWIGHT YORKE
Newcastle (a) 3-4
September 1997

DION DUBLIN
Southampton (a) 4-1
November 1998

...AND THREE IN THE CUPS!

STAN COLLYMORE
Stromsgodset (a) 3-0
(UEFA Cup, round 1)
September 1998

BENITO CARBONE
Leeds (h) 3-2
(FA Cup, round 5)
January 2000

JUAN PABLO ANGEL
Wycombe (a) 5-0
(League Cup, round 2)
September 2003

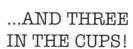

CRAIG IN
the spotlight

Footballers often say they don't read what's written about them in newspapers but Craig Gardner couldn't wait to see how he had been depicted in a book called _The Team_.

When he was interviewed by author Mick Dennis, Craig was still an Academy player and, having been put out of action by an injury, was anxious about his future.

But by the time the book was published, though, the midfielder from Yardley had broken into the first team and had made several Premiership appearances.

Even so, he was delighted to be the subject of a chapter entitled The Academy Player in a book which looks at all aspects of football.

As a result of that project, Craig was subsequently asked to appear on a **Match of the Day** item about the Premier League's Reading Stars scheme.

And he admits the experience, which unfolded in the quiet seclusion of Villa's dressing room, was even more nerve-racking than stepping out onto the pitch in front of thousands of spectators.

"I'd rather play in front of a capacity crowd than go through that again," he said after being in the full glare of the BBC camera lights.

"I was really nervous, sitting there waiting to be interviewed. But it wasn't too bad once we got going."

"I'd rather play in front of a capacity crowd than go through that again"

BARRY

Gareth **Barry**

SPOT THE BALL

Using your football skills, can you spot where the ball is in this picture?

SPOT THE DIFFERENCE

There are six differences in the pictures below, can you spot what they are?

See page 60 for the answers.

Can you help Kevin Phillips get to his football through this maze? Use your finger to find your way. Answer on p60 to p61.

42

A game to remember

HOW THE TABLE LOOKED

	P	W	D	L	F	A	Pts
VILLA	10	6	3	1	17	12	21
Leeds Utd.	10	5	5	0	13	4	20
Arsenal	10	5	4	1	19	7	19
Liverpool	9	6	1	2	17	9	19
Man Utd.	10	4	3	3	27	17	18

Younger supporters may find it difficult to imagine Villa sitting on the top of the table, but it happened a few years ago – for one week only.

In October 2001, the boys in claret and blue surged to the Premiership summit with an exciting 3-2 Villa Park victory over Bolton Wanderers.

Villa had started the season impressively, drawing away to Tottenham and at home to Manchester United before notching an excellent 3-1 victory at Liverpool.

After being held to a goalless home draw by Sunderland, they then won 3-1 at Southampton before beating both Blackburn Rovers and Fulham 2-0 in consecutive home matches.

That took them to fourth, but they suffered a setback in a 3-2 defeat at Everton – where Peter Schmeichel became the only goalkeeper in the club's history to score a competitive goal.

But Villa were back on home soil for the next two fixtures, and they took full advantage. They beat Charlton 1-0 with a Hassan Kachloul goal in midweek, and were in third place as they lined up against Bolton.

There didn't seem much prospect of climbing to the top when former Walsall striker Michael Ricketts put the visitors ahead after only two minutes.

Bolton had beaten Manchester United at Old Trafford the previous

week, so Villa clearly had a battle on their hands, but they responded perfectly, Juan Pablo Angel soared in a crowded goalmouth to head a 13th minute equaliser.

Villa then took control, although they had to wait until three minutes before half-time to take the lead, Angel's flicking setting up Darius Vassell for a low 15-yard shot just inside the right hand post.

Within a minute of the second half, it was 3-1 when Villa were awarded a penalty and Angel converted the spot kick for his second goal.

The game was far from over, though, and Villa endured some anxious moments after Ricketts had scored a second for Bolton in the 75th minute. But the final whistle was greeted by loud chanting from the Holte End: "We are top of the league!"

MATCH DETAILS
FA Premiership
27th October 2001

VILLA 3
BOLTON 2
Villa goals: Angel 13, 46 pen; Vassell 42. Bolton goals: Ricketts 2, 75.
Villa line-up: Schmeichel; Delaney, Alpay, Staunton, Wright; Hadji, Hendrie, Boateng, Kachloul; Angel, Vassell. Subs: Dublin (for Angel, 72), Merson (for Vassell, 73), Taylor (for Hendrie, 86).

BOUMA

Wilfred Bouma

What's YOUR name?

Sometimes, people name their children after their football favourites – and sometimes it happens by accident!

Last season, for instance, we became aware of two young Villa supporters with names which may be familiar to you – Aaron Hughes and Doug Ellis.

Eight-year-old Aaron, from Castle Bromwich, wasn't named after the Northern Ireland defender, who joined Villa in the summer of 2005.

The youngster, in fact, was just a little put out about our £1m signing from Newcastle United – because he'd dreamed of being the first Aaron Hughes to play for Villa!

"Obviously that can't happen now," says Aaron's dad Neil. "But Aaron was thrilled at meeting his namesake."

Doug Ellis was equally delighted when he attended his first match at Villa Park – and met Doug Ellis.

Young Doug, from Essex, is only seven, but he shares his name with Villa's chairman. His dad,

Doug meets Doug

Aaron meets Aaron

Rob, isn't really a football fan, and didn't realise the coincidence. But his uncle Martyn certainly did – he's a Villa season ticket holder.

And where did Doug sit for his first Villa game? The Doug Ellis stand, of course!

FIRST KITS!

Villa's players proudly wear the club's traditional claret and blue shirt, but how would they look in the replica kits of the teams they supported when they were growing up? We present YOUR favourites in the colours of THEIR favourites – although Gavin McCann insists he is really a Blackpool fan. He was given his Saints shirt by a cousin!

Top: WILFRED BOUMA – PSV Eindhoven, GARETH BARRY – Tottenham, CRAIG GARDNER – Villa, STUART TAYLOR – West Ham.
Bottom: STEVEN DAVIS – Rangers, GAVIN McCANN – Southampton, KEVIN PHILLIPS – England, LIAM RIDGEWELL – Liverpool, GARY CAHILL – Sheffield Wednesday.

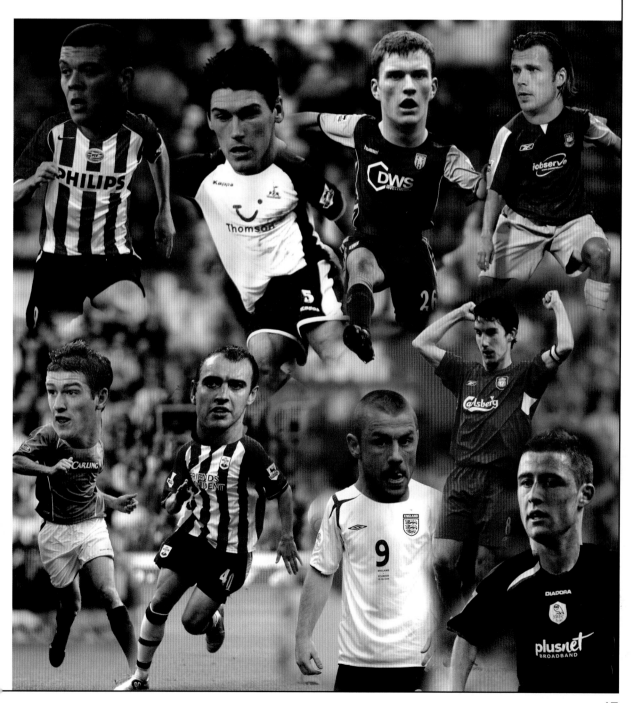

Junior

FUN, FUN, FUN

Football is the most important thing on the agenda at Villa Park – but the club are always looking for ways of entertaining our younger fans.

When we staged a Family Fun Day last season, for instance, it was a huge success. For one day only, Villa supporters were able to sit in the lower section of the North Stand, which is

NOT JUST WILLIAM

Not all Villa fans live in the Midlands. Some of you travel long distances to cheer on the boys in claret and blue.

Little William Johnson, for instance, is brought to Villa Park by his dad Graham – all the way from Redruth in Cornwall.

William won a free Junior Villans membership at a Family Fun Day organised by the South West Villans Supporters' Club and as you can see, part of his welcome pack included a large hand.

Also pictured is Villa marketing executive Dan Meredith.

I'M THE BOSS!

Jade Vaughan would love to have a go at being a manager – so when she was a mascot at one of our home matches, we gave her the chance to see how it might feel!

Jade's hobbies include football and reading, and she also enjoys talking a lot. Just like a football manager!

usually reserved for visiting fans.

Admission prices were reduced for that part of the ground, and it was packed out as mums and dads brought along the kids to enjoy pre-match and half-time entertainment provided by a stilt walker, a novelty balloon maker and a magician.

The fans verdict? Just magic!

Villans

VILLANS AND HAMMERS

What's all this? A young Villan and a young Hammer – being kept a safe distance apart by an Oldham supporter!

The man in the middle is Roger Winter, who started supporting Oldham when he worked there.

He now lives in Sutton Coldfield, so it was no great surprise when his son Edward pledged his allegiance to Villa. But Edward's younger brother Toby decided to support West Ham after watching them on television last season.

So now Roger has to act as referee when the boys start arguing about their favourite teams!

LET'S FACE IT...

How's this for a true Villan? Jordan Goodridge from Rowley Regis proudly displays the face-painting makeover she underwent before a game at Villa Park. When you're devoted to a club, they say you wear your heart on your sleeve. Jordan clearly prefers to wear Villa's badge on her face!

Which one's for YOU?

Junior Villans is the club for all claret and blue nuts up to the age of 16.
Check out the section for your age group (or get mum or dad to do it for you) and make sure you don't miss out on the goodies on offer.

VILLA CUBS

Pre-school Villans (from birth to five) can enroll in the Villa Cubs and receive a welcome pack which includes a colouring book, a pencil case with crayons, and a sticker book.

VILLA LIONS

Six-to-12-year olds receive a wristband, a lunch box, a mini scarf pennant and a fan horn to make sure you're never ignored – either at Villa Park or at home!

VILLA TEENS

The "cool" club for fans between the ages of 13 and 16 offers a wristband, a computer mouse and an Aston Villa mouse mat.

Membership for any of the three clubs runs for 12 months from your date of enrolment.

In addition to your "welcome gifts", members of all three clubs receive a personalised membership card, exclusive newsletters throughout the season, a Christmas card and gift, plus a 10 per cent discount on goods in our stores at the Villa Village or Pavilion Central.

There's also the chance to 'Meet the Players' in one of our great competitions, plus free admission to reserve home games. – and all Junior Villans can go free to our popular Kickin' Kids parties.

To enroll, call 0871 423 8101, or e-mail hercules@avfc.co.uk.

QUIZ TIME

MINI SOCCER-DU

The Sudoku craze has swept the nation over the past couple of years – so we've devised our own version, specially aimed at young Villa fans. Instead of using numbers, we've used Villa legends who made their names in shirts with a particular number. Fill in the squares in the grid so that each row, column and each of the 3 x 3 squares contains all the names.

If it makes it easier, simply switch the names for numbers:

1- Nigel SPINK, 2 - Stan LYNN,
3 - Charlie AITKEN, 4 - Allan EVANS,
5 - Paul McGRATH, 6 - Dennis MORTIMER

DOT-TO-DOT
Join the dots, in number order to reveal your favourite Villa mascot.

SPINK	EVANS			MORTIMER	
	LYNN			McGRATH	
LYNN		SPINK		AITKEN	
		MORTIMER		EVANS	McGRATH

THE NAME GAME

Unravel these anagrams to reveal the names of Villa players:

1. ROB IS L.A. MAN!
2. SAVED IN VEST
3. A HILLY CRAG
4. CRADING CARER
5. AHA! BIG ROLL ON BARGE

TRACK DOWN THE SQUAD!

Here's a chance to test your knowledge of last season's Villa squad. A total of 14 names are hidden in our word search. Some are horizontal, some are vertical, some go backwards and one is diagonal. The names you should find are:

AGBONLAHOR	ANGEL
BARRY	BAROS
BERGER	BOUMA
CAHILL	DAVIS
GARDNER	HUGHES
McCANN	MOORE
RIDGEWELL	SORENSEN

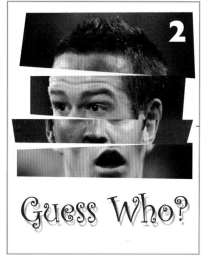

V	I	N	E	S	N	E	R	O	S
D	L	M	C	C	A	N	N	B	T
A	G	B	O	N	L	A	H	O	R
V	E	A	Y	R	R	A	B	U	E
I	M	R	R	E	R	O	O	M	G
S	Y	O	T	D	W	H	J	A	R
Q	X	S	O	A	N	G	E	L	E
U	R	H	U	G	H	E	S	L	B
C	A	H	I	L	L	Z	R	D	C
A	L	L	E	W	E	G	D	I	R

Answers on page 61

51

Lions' rhymes!

We all learned nursery rhymes as we were growing up, and lifelong Villa fan BRENDA HUGHES was no exception. But Brenda has rewritten some of her favourites to give them a claret and blue theme!

Mary had a little lamb

Mary had a little friend
His scarf was claret and blue
And everywhere that Mary went
Her little friend went, too
He taught her all the football songs
And joy was ever bringing
They often sat in Aston Park
To hear the Holte End singing.

There was a crooked man

There was a crooked man
Who walked a crooked mile
He found himself by Villa Park
And wore a crooked smile
He bought a Villa hat
And a scarf that bore the name
But forgot to buy a ticket
So he couldn't watch the game!

Jack and Jill

Jack and Jill went up the hill
To see the Villa play
Jack said to Jill 'It's such a thrill
It's hard to keep away'
Off went Jack but soon came back
With season tickets for two
And now the pair are always there
Watching the claret and blue!

There was an old woman

There was an old woman who lived in a shoe
Had so many children in claret and blue
She gave them all money in margarine tubs
Then sent them to Aston to join Villa cubs

Little Miss Muffet

Little Miss Muffet sat on a tuffet
Reading the Claret & Blue
It wasn't the spider that sat down beside her
But other folk reading it, too!

Doctor Foster

Doctor Foster came from Gloucester
A Villa game to see
Sat in the North Stand
Said 'My, this is grand
But I wish I could get in for free.'

Baa baa black sheep

Baa baa black sheep,
Will the Villa win?
Yes sir, yes sir, three goals in
One from the corner,
One from the spot
And one from the striker,
Whose name I forgot!

Little boy (Claret &) Blue

Litlle boy blue come blow your horn
Your shirt is ragged, your trousers are torn
So get off to Villa and buy something new
You'll look very smart in claret and blue.

Little boy blue come blow your horn
To be a young Villa fan you were born
So join with the Lions and start life anew
'Cause you are the little boy claret and blue

Golden Moments

There hasn't been a great deal of silverware around Villa Park in recent times, but the year 2007 marks two very special anniversaries for the club.

It's 25 years since the greatest achievement in the club's history – when we lifted the prestigious European Cup – and 50 years since our last FA Cup triumph.

Needless to say, captains Dennis Mortimer and Johnny Dixon were bursting with pride as they lifted the respective trophies, Mortimer in Rotterdam and Dixon at Wembley.

And what made the two victories even sweeter was that Villa were very much the underdogs on both occasions.

In the 1982 European Cup final, they were 1-0 winners against German giants Bayern Munich, one of the top club sides in the world at that time. And the team's opponents in the 1957 FA Cup final were mighty Manchester United, the famous "Busby Babes."

Strangely enough, both finals were affected – in different ways – by injuries to goalkeepers.

At Wembley in 1957, United 'keeper Ray Wood was carried off following a nasty sixth minute collision with Villa's Irish international Peter McParland.

There were no substitutes allowed in those days, so Jackie Blanchflower went in goal – and was beaten by two second half goals from McParland which gave Villa a 2-1 win.

In the 1982 European final, it was Villa who lost their goalkeeper early in the match, Jimmy Rimmer having to go off with a neck injury.

But substitute 'keeper Nigel Spink, who had played hardly any first team football, went on and made himself one of Villa's heroes with some outstanding saves.

The other hero? Peter Withe – the man who scored Villa's winning goal!

Happy Golden Anniversary to the boys of '57 – and happy Silver Anniversary to the boys of '82!

1982 European Cup final - Peter Withe celebrates with Gary Shaw

Oi Ref!
Gimme-a-break-cheesecake

Here's a recipe which has a Villa flavour – and is also very tasty!

You will need:

4 digestive biscuits
1 pack cream cheese
1 tablespoon sugar
2 tablespoons blackberries or blueberries (mashed with a fork)
4 tablespoons raspberries
(1 teaspoon grated lemon rind, if you wish)

What to do:

Put the cream cheese into a bowl.

Add the sugar and mashed fruit (plus lemon rind, if you've used it).

Mix well until the mixture turns blue, and the sugar has dissolved.

Spread a thick layer of the mixture onto each biscuit.

Top with a layer of raspberries. Chill in the fridge for 2 hours. Enjoy with your friends!

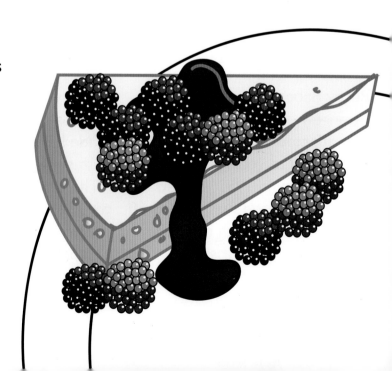

WHO SAID IT?

Can you identify Villa's players by the things they said last season? To give you a start, the first comment was made by goalkeeper Thomas Sorensen so the answer is 1A. See if you can match the others!

1 I have my theory about preventing people scoring from penalties but I'm not going to say what it is!

2 It's not easy to leave Liverpool but Villa are also a big club so I was happy to come here.

3 I had some great years at Newcastle but there comes a time when you have to move on. I've come to Villa because it's a big club with good players.

4 It was great to score a hat-trick but it would be wrong for me to be anything but level-headed.

5 I joined PSV when I was 12 and I haven't known anything else. It's the first time in my career that I've been away from home.

6 A friend of mine sent me a text message saying I give away more pens than W.H.Smith!

7 It was the first time I've scored with a header and it was nice to get my first derby goal.

8 To have made 300 appearances for Villa before my 25th birthday is a big achievement.

9 I enjoy my football and I just get on with it.

10 All the lads I went to school with are Villa fans and when I speak to them I can't believe I'm here.

THE PLAYERS

A	THOMAS SORENSEN
B	WILFRED BOUMA
C	GARETH BARRY
D	AARON HUGHES
E	CRAIG GARDNER
F	GAVIN McCANN
G	LIAM RIDGEWELL
H	LUKE MOORE
I	STEVEN DAVIS
J	MILAN BAROS

Answers on pages 61

57

Away the lads!

1992-93   1993-94

Villa's players don't always step out in the club's traditional claret and blue. When the team are away and their colours clash with the opposition, they have to change – and the club's "away kit" has certainly been varied in recent times.

During the Premiership years, the team's away colours have changed annually. But the colour scheme of white shirts and light blue shirts has emerged as the most predominant kit – and the lads are back in white for the current campaign.

Three of the players, in fact, had a sneak preview of the 2006-07 away kit at the end of last season when they agreed to model it for the club's merchandising catalogue. Gareth Barry, Liam Ridgewell and goalkeeper Thomas Sorensen were the men in question – and they gave the thumbs-up to being back in white.

"The design is really smart," said Gareth. "The lads will be more than happy with it."

The shirt features a subtle claret and blue trim – plus the name of Villa's new sponsor, the internet gaming company 32RED.com, together with small emblems of hearts, clubs, diamonds and spades.

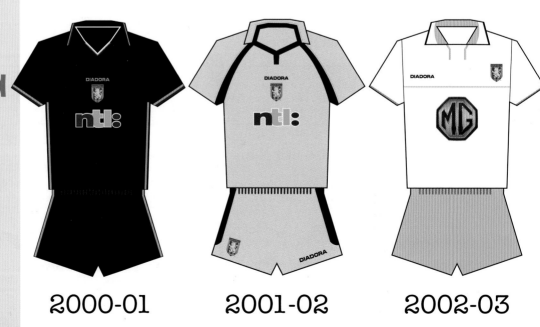

2000-01   2001-02   2002-03

1994-95

1995-96

1996-97

1997-98

1998-99

1999-00

2003-04

2004-05

2005-06

Spot the ball p33

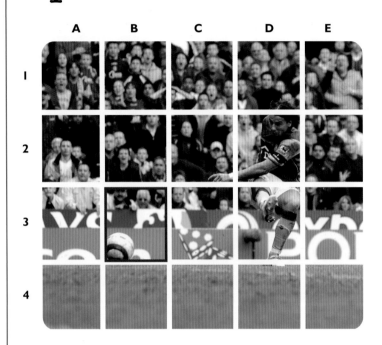

Spot the ball p41

SPOT THE DIFFERENCE

1. H of holte end is missing.

2. E on end is filled in.

3. H of the is missing.

4. One stand is green.

5. The grass is blue.

6. The birds in the sky.

Answers to p41.

GET ON?

MINI SOCCER-DU

Answers to p50.

SPINK	EVANS	McGRATH	AITKEN	MORTIMER	LYNN
MORTIMER	LYNN	AITKEN	EVANS	McGRATH	SPINK
McGRATH	AITKEN	EVANS	SPINK	LYNN	MORTIMER
LYNN	MORTIMER	SPINK	McGRATH	AITKEN	EVANS
EVANS	McGRATH	LYNN	MORTIMER	SPINK	AITKEN
AITKEN	SPINK	MORTIMER	LYNN	EVANS	McGRATH

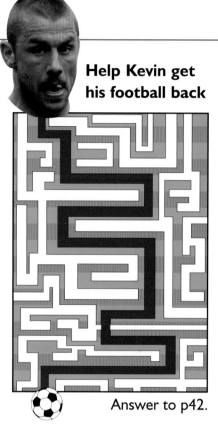

Help Kevin get his football back

Answer to p42.

TRACK DOWN THE SQUAD!

V	I	N	E	S	N	E	R	O	S
D	L	M	C	C	A	N	N	B	T
A	G	B	O	N	L	A	H	O	R
V	E	A	Y	R	R	A	B	U	E
I	M	R	R	E	R	O	O	M	G
S	Y	O	T	D	W	H	J	A	R
Q	X	S	O	A	N	G	E	L	E
U	R	H	U	G	H	E	S	L	B
C	A	H	I	L	D	Z	R	D	C
A	L	L	E	W	E	G	D	I	R

Answers to p51.

THE NAME GAME

1. Milan Baros
2. Steven Davis
3. Gary Cahill
4. Craig Gardner
5. Gabriel Agbonlahor

Answers to p50.

WHO SAID THAT?

1A, 2J, 3D, 4H, 5B
6G, 7I, 8C, 9F, 10E.

Answers to p57.

GUESS WHO?

1. Juan Pablo Angel.
2. Hair - Gary Cahill, Eyes - Steven Davis, Nose - Gavin McCann, Lips - Graig Gardner.
3. Gareth Barry.

Answers to p51.